Never Obituary

Stacie Mahaffey

BookLeaf
Publishing

Presentation by *BookLeaf Publishing*

Web: www.bookleafpub.com

E-mail: info@bookleafpub.com

ISBN: 9789357748858

First edition 2023

DEDICATION

To all the women who feel they've lost their
voice in the face of adversity or drowned their
spirit in domesticated pretense. May you
discover the power within to harness your

strength and slay your giants.

ACKNOWLEDGEMENT

I would like to thank my creator: "I will praise You, for I am fearfully and wonderfully made; Marvelous are Your works, And that my soul knows very well." Psalm 139:14

PREFACE

My name, Stacie, means "resurrection," and I have come back after many types of deaths to be reborn even stronger; knowing more while holding on to less.

I won't describe my hopes and dreams and whether they are now ghosts or weeds I desperately try to pluck from an overgrown garden.

Blindfolded, I have even followed some through the trenches of hell, telling myself it was probably just too sunny along the way before the mirage mercifully unveiled itself. It was as though I was at the altar of a barren god, whereupon I had offered up nearly every part of my heart with no hope of ever seeing a return.

Instead of fear, came opportunity. Blazing fire burns away the old for clearer paths to unfold. Like a snake shedding her skin, I learned the art of detachment, setting the stage for things anew.

On occasion, I'm the initiator, slowly starting only sparkles, but what's relevant, is a reign on that fire, to absolutely hold on to my ability to diffuse it. If I were to pour myself in with abandon, I would be left only to find myself again in the ashes.

Nevertheless, I'm alive, bearing witness to events as they unfold; sometimes gracefully, sometimes audaciously.

Awake

The instant it clicks, my brain pushes through to
the next level, shredding the fog like useless
mail when they've already emailed me.
Wasting trees.
Who has the audacity to be so appallingly
redundant?
A waste of a sacred span of time.
It was MINE, not theirs.

Get ready for the deal of a lifetime?
I am ready.
I am ready for anything life deals ME.
I was ready before they cut down those
oxygen-producing trees for a garden sale.

Life is the sum of cliched seasons.
People welcome the winds they cursed months
before.
Why should I panic?

I make every step count,
instead of fumbling and stumbling as
they accumulate cheap medals for good
intentions.
"At least you tried," they'll say.

Laughing will make them feel better, but I'm
done with A-Z before they've posted a selfie
with a label
that outshines their personality

Warning: Narcissus never left the pool

Sometimes I have so many balls rolling,
I lose track and later find that I've created an
avalanche before noon.
Maybe it will knock some of them into
consciousness.

I AM awake and
the world is turning
I'm allowed to fuel
what should be burning
I'll light a match so quickly
they'll catch a dream
before it's forgotten
too many times
the ripe become too rotten
act fast, think later
it won't last
get it while it's there
don't find yourself
in a thoughtless stare

Carbon Copy Heart

It's always called a new start,
writing on the carbon copy of my heart.
He may trace the path from when the ink was
new, when there was room to breathe amidst the
wet blue

I'll respond politely,
stifling every laugh or wince,
As if I haven't read this line
Or had a thought since!
I'll say it's too wordy,
when in fact, I am bored.
After scripted salutations and
 temptations,
 I may toss it on the floor.

If he's efficient with his allotted space,
awing me with a new creation,
 the page will show its scars
as the pen leaves its marks of careful navigation.
It might look like a cluster,
so the key is distraction.
I'll try to look for more room
if he can be pleased with his fraction.

This Glass

When the wine is poured in,
watch this glass as it fills.

Embracing every drop,
this glass stands still

If the wine sparkles,
does its new vessel react?
Does it bend, tremble,
or begin to crack?
As your thirst gives way
to a taste so sweet,
does a firmer grip split
this glass your lips meet?

Even while empty,
this glass will shine,
and it will never beg you
to pour more wine.

A Will

I was given a will
not only of stealth
one that unceasingly sheds the debt
so I can neglect to remember
what you choose to regret

you are weak

I'm untying

the last knot

I am flying

you will fall

until you let your wounds clot

Do You Remember?

Do you remember?
The grass was green upon paths unseen and the
world still held all its splendor?

Do you remember?
When chance and potential burst with buzzing
sparks and flew with each handful?

Do you remember?
When hopes were sewn upon nothing but the
smallest shimmer?

Do you remember?
Before when buckets of rain fell,
we'd dance to its cadences

Now we need a weather prediction app to
suggest we dress in ways that prevent us from
being harmed by mere mist
and an acquaintance to agree it's safe to call that
gentle, glistening bead on your cheek
a drop of rain.

Deconstruction

The truth was there far before
This light burned your eyes.

Too afraid, you looked away
For the darkest places to hide

Now darkness withers away
At your memories of the sun

Whether or not you know
The beginning has begun

You're stumbling in the dark
Maybe when too many times
You have fell

You'll grow wise
and realize
That you built your own hell

Cold Shadows

If I blossomed, you were the sun,
surging with warmth after
every delayed dawn.

I searchingly spread my roots and carefully
opened every pressed petal
until I completely surrendered my bursting ring
of winsome pursuers to your sustaining
emanation.

Embedded into the ground,
I could still acclimate on dull, dark days.
Turning, twisting, searching.

But, unlike the butterfly,
I could not leap or dance out of the forsaken
shadows to chase down your rays.

A product of my environment,
I could only thrive where my roots lay.

Old Friend

You've done everything right
I smile at my scars and laugh at my uncanny
ability to harness chaos.
I have more wild stories than you have excuses
as to why
you still can't meet for lunch.

Eruption

Humming along the ceiling,
crawling like snakes,
distractions shriek like an impatient alarm you
made for an appointment last week.

The drive to push yourself
isn't there like it once was.

Under pressure, things collapse,
but this vessel isn't hollow.

Equal amounts of forces dwell within
In conflict or in harmony,
they'll rise to the surface after being submerged;
buzzing and building until meeting an outside
force with equal fervor,
like shooting a missile into a volcano
on the brink of eruption.

There's not a word that reflects amusement
coupled with anger and apathy.

One More Glimpse

Your eyes were not
blue as the sea

where depth is measured

No

They were reflections of an infinite sky

On cloudy days,
I did my best to learn their language
Shivering in shadows
Observing shapes
Guessing at interpretation

I camped through shaking storms
Sometimes
Without shelter
Sometimes
I summoned your electricity
on clear days
for either
one more glimpse of radiance

or a quick shock
teeming with rebuke

You said I was chasing dragons

On nights of glory
I was hypnotized,
wrapped in a legion of luminary guides

Blinded by the supernova,
there is a trail
 I continue to hunt for

The Fortress

The bricks are going up

The fortress will be sealed

I offered peace

I offered compromise

You respect nothing

And ensure your own demise

To Aphrodite, Goddess of Love

I only took a sip of your honeyed tea
Before I flew above this tree

Underneath a star that fell
And over the moon behind a comet's tail!

I felt the pleasant surprise
Of electric wonder in another's eyes

Then too soon the death of a blossom
So many times, the wonder forgotten.

But below without even a wing,
I have a voice that will sing

"No longer will I follow
Trails of sparkles
with no fire tomorrow
I'll rest in laughter at birds lost in the breeze,
So count your fools and keep your tea!"

Seeking Proper Translator

I am full of electricity and by God,
I feel it pulsate through me constantly.

At times, it's as if I grabbed a rod and climbed
the highest tree.

I've never located a proper translator for these
sparkling thoughts,
but they shock and dazzle in the places you least
expect them to.

It's so easy to be misunderstood by those who
can't feel the subtle tension.

I'll wait for someone to come out for the light
show or two,
but I'll let down anyone expecting a
multi-colored mirage.

Run

Hell on wheels.
Running away from what I possibly need.
Defying stability, resisting permanent ground.

My feet will not be cast in concrete here.

Running towards uncertainty.
If I stop, I might see how lost I really am.

I don't want to know.

Kick up my heels
Never letting the dust settle
You can't see where I'm going

That's how I like it

There's no time to look back

So what I leave behind
Is unclear anyhow

Before that storm comes
I'll be gone

Before the lightning and rain
Chase me down

So I look for the sign and run

Forbidding the chaotic wind
From carrying me to unknown ground

The roses smell so sweet
I want to pick them

Forgetting how thorns make me bleed

Once again
Weakness allows fate to prevail

I've been swept up into the eye
Of the storm's uncompromising twist

Suddenly I arrive
To a place I didn't know I missed

Refuge

Offerings of peace
Thrown back like spoiled meat
Can't they smell?

The green grass must be cut
Those unbridled dominant whims
Savagely steal the sunlight

Insulate the keep

In a cocoon of stone,
These petals shall unfold

Coping Mechanisms

They said, "be yourself,"
But "don't cast pearls before swine."
So I stay apart
after I take what's mine.
Look up
 look closely.
Why should I make a crutch
when they clearly can see?

You see, I'm not any closer to a revelation;
I'm still wondering where my knots are too tight.

I'm gasping, but it's not from strangulation,
just from a thought before it's been made right.

Because under these wheels that turn,
plays a tune that earns
its own meals just for the tone
it sets for the fight:

"You'll never remember this tomorrow,
but no one else's to be blamed for your sorrow.
What a waste of time
it is to build a shrine

to an evil never thought of
until you made it so."

So, I let'em see a smile that escapes their fear;
a smile that's known no pain.
Just like the bastards they are,
I don't even give my tears a name.

Telehumans

Is our flesh and blood too wild to free?
These walls are tall,
and filtered thoughts our electricity.

Intention is a shade staler than a try.
We dream before we awake,
can we just do it without always saying why?

Do we actually need approval or a reward to
give?
If we only reach out with the tips of our hands,
then when do we truly live?

The Long Con

A close comfort,
that truly was the sharpest knife.

Now I return to that empty alley.

Your heart betrays you
Don't you remember?

Mortal love.

Merely sprinkles for our parched souls.

It can't even be rationed.

Intuitive Piracy

Shall I drag the waters some more?

I braved the wave

To dive deep and blind

Scratching the ocean floor,

Terror or treasure I'd find

Do my senses contradict?

You're a liar, or I'm a bitch.

The Machine

Quick clicks
And slick tricks
Foster this blossoming mirage
Held up only by continued sacrifices of our time

To stop? Would you truly live?

Eyes Down
Hands wrapped around concerns
Out of context and your realm

Too far and wide, you cast your net

Never realizing the prize is right before you.

Waste no energy on perfection
This semblance of being unscathed leaves us
weak

Scars and sins make us mortal

There are so many ways you'll fail
trying to connect to a machine.

Always

Mischievously elegant

Observations and companionships
kept at a cautiously, calculated distance

The meeting's on her terms.

Superfluous affections and inhibitions of her
freedom
Are put out with her claws
—and anything else she's testing.
Always.

Printed in the USA
CPSIA information can be obtained
at www.ICGtesting.com
LVHW060352100823
754636LV00016B/989